KARATE

KARATE

Steve Arneil (7th Dan)
Liam Keaveney (3rd Dan)

TEACH YOURSELF BOOKS

Long-renowned as *the* authoritative source for self-guided learning – with more than 30 million copies sold worldwide – the *Teach Yourself* series includes over 200 titles in the fields of languages, crafts, hobbies, sports, and other leisure activities.

British Library Cataloguing in Publication Data
Keaveney, Liam
  Teach yourself karate. – New ed. – (TY series)
  I. Title II. Arneil, S. III. Series
  796.8153

Library of Congress Catalog Card Number: 92-82516

First published in UK 1991 by Hodder Headline Plc, 338 Euston Road,
London NW1 3BH

First published in US 1993 by NTC Publishing Group, 4255 West Touhy Avenue,
Lincolnwood (Chicago), Illinois 60646 – 1975 U.S.A.

Typeset by Rowland Phototypesetting Ltd, Bury St Edmunds.
Printed in Great Britain by Cox & Wyman Ltd, Reading, Berkshire.

14   13   12   11   10   9   8   7   6
1999   1998   1997   1996   1995   1994

Contents

1

History and Origins of Karate

- The birth of Karate
- Weapons in Karate
- The main concepts
- The route to power

The birth of Karate

Gichin Funakoshi introduced the basic concept of Karate into Japan from Okinawa in 1916 and, particularly since the 1960s, the popularity of Karate has been increasing rapidly.

The earliest origins of Karate as we know it today are somewhat vague due to a lack of documentation. The traditional idea accepted by most authorities is that it started in India. A Buddhist priest, called in Chinese *Daruma* (or *Bohodidarma*, as he is better known), wished to take his particular sect of Buddhism, called Zen, to the Chinese as a missionary venture. It was not uncommon for itinerant priests to be able to fight, as they would frequently be in danger on their wanderings from wild animals as well as men. Even Gautama Sidartha himself had been a warrior before he became the Buddha. When he established Buddhism, he saw no contradiction in the idea of a man of peace and love also being skilful in combat.

In about AD 500, Bhodidarma reached the court of Emperor Wu at Chein-K'ang in China, where he was warmly received. He left the courts, eventually heading north to Henan Province and into seclusion in the Shaolin temple ('Shorin' in Japanese) to teach Zen. He also taught his system of unarmed combat called Shorin Kempo.

Forms of Chinese combat have been recorded as far back as 3000 BC. Bhodidarma is credited with being the founder of Chinese Kempo, mainly because he added the meditative practices of Yoga and Zen, making it a more complete system, as we know it today. Zen is inseparably linked with Karate and every Master of Karate seeks a more enlightened experience by studying Zen; in fact, all the major developments in Shorin Kempo were achieved by various priests, through the years. Finally, the close connection between priests and medicine resulted in the discovery not only of vital spots on the human body where cures could be applied, but also spots where Kempo attacks could be directed for the best results.

From China, Kempo spread north to Mongolia, east to Korea and south-east to Okinawa. Eventually it reached Japan, where it became extremely popular after the Kamakura era (about AD 1200). The soldier class, the Samurai, in particular welcomed both the combat forms and the Zen philosophy. The morality and mysticism of Zen Buddhism appealed to their sensibilities, but the real attraction was the way it provided them with a discipline which made them capable of great endurance and excellence in fighting, by giving them the special psychological skills and insights into both themselves and their opponents.

At various times in history – for instance in 1400 and again in 1609, in Okinawa – the authorities forbade the populace to use arms. As a means of protection against the bandits, and sometimes even against the authorities, unarmed combat became widely taught. The schools, themselves usually confined to the temples, were nevertheless kept secret, because if discovered they would have been immediately wiped out by those in power.

It was not until 1901 that Karate, as we now know it, was brought out of secret study and taught openly in Okinawa. In 1916, Master Gichin Funakoshi came from Okinawa to Tokyo and pioneered the modern system of Karate in Japan. Born from many origins, there are today many schools of Karate, each with its own merits and perhaps its own faults.

The word Karate, in its literal translation, means 'empty hand'.

Weapons in Karate

The principal 'weapons' of Karate are the hands and feet, and we will deal more comprehensively with these in a later chapter. However, the competent student using these weapons does not rely on them alone. For example, in using the fist as a weapon, it is essential that the *karateka* also makes use of the wrist, arm, elbow, shoulder and hips – in effect the entire body is used in delivering an attack with the fist. It can also be seen that in using our feet as a Karate weapon, we must rely on the ankle, knee, thigh and hips working together. It is therefore correct to say that the entire body must be trained and correctly co-ordinated in order to make effective and efficient use of the Karate weapons.

In physical terms, Karate training not only conditions the body and improves speed, strength and co-ordination, it also develops the student's alertness and self awareness. As a result the student may experience a development of self-confidence – a confidence in ability in relation to the world around him/her. It is no surprise that with this self-confidence, not to be confused with brashness or arrogance, the student can also experience a degree of inner peace and calmness.

The essence of Karate is perseverance, in techniques and in practice. Success will not come in days or months – it will perhaps take many years. The mysticism of Karate is a worldwide phenomenon. What is it that gives the experienced *karateka* the ability and power to break bricks and so on with such ease? Quite simply, in terms of physical properties power is related to speed.

The main concepts

There are certain factors which are important in maximising the *karateka*'s ability in applying Karate techniques. These are as follows:

Striking
The striking part of the body should be as small as possible. For example, the *seiken* (forefist) should be used when punching – not all the knuckles though, so that you provide the object you are striking with the least amount of surface area to resist (Fig. 1). This is not a general rule but it applies to certain techniques – your little finger has a small striking area, but it would be impractical to attempt to hit anyone with it and expect an effective attack, because

it is not powerful. Conversely, an arrow is more effective than an iron bar (Fig. 1).

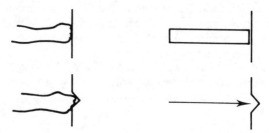

Fig.1

Power

Power is also an extremely important factor – you must be able to generate maximum power in your technique given your physical limitations. For example, in order to maximise the effect, you must generate more power by putting your whole body behind your punch (for example using a full hip movement).

Speed

Speed also is very important if you are to maximise the effect of any technique. Remember that if, for example, you attempt to break any object (i.e. *tameshiwari*) speed is very important – hitting an object slowly, (as in Fig. 2b) even if you are strong, does not transmit the same power as if you executed the technique quickly (as in Fig. 2a).

To illustrate this, imagine a *karateka* weighing 100 Kg and

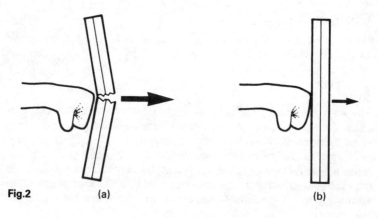

Fig.2   (a)   (b)

standing on the ground on one foot – the ground he is standing on receives a direct force of 100 Kg. Now if the *karateka* jumps up into the air and lands on the same foot, the force will be greater than the original 100 Kg, due to the acceleration caused by gravity.

The route to power

In order to generate applied power effectively, the student must understand the various steps of progressive development, explained briefly below:

Position
The student should have a good theoretical and practical knowledge of the Karate stances and techniques.

Balance
This is the means by which the student controls the actual body position of his or her body when it is both stationary and moving.

Co-ordination
This is what enables the student to execute the various techniques with controlled balance in a given position.

Form
The student can develop form by executing all the techniques with good position, balance and co-ordination.

Speed
This is where the student increases the rhythm of performance without any loss of form.

Power
Power is the strengthening of the techniques.

Reflex
Having successfully understood and developed all the above steps, the student will reach a stage, through constant repetition, whereby the techniques become a natural movement.

It must be emphasised that the student should not rush this learning process and should, as far as possible, establish and understand each individual movement and in addition should take care that he or she understands the meaning of the technique.

2

General Procedures and Conditioning Exercises

- Joining a club
- Club etiquette and procedure
- Gradings
- The bowing procedure

- The kneeling procedure
- Conditioning exercises
- Stretching
- Breathing

Joining a club

Clubs in general

It must be emphasised that you cannot successfully learn Karate solely from the contents of a book. If possible, you should seek out and join a respectable and established club or *dojo*. Conscious of the fact that this book has worldwide circulation, we will not go into detail on specific facts relating to nationally recognised bodies and organisations.

Having decided you wish to learn Karate you will realise that there are many differing styles of Karate taught throughout the world. Some examples of these are *Kyokushinkai*, *Shotokan*, *Wado-Ryu*, and *Goju*, but there are several more. Each holds and teaches the same basic principles of Karate, but conversely each has an independent philosophical ideal, and methods of teaching and competition differ from club to club. It should also be said that each has its own advantages and disadvantages to the individual wishing to learn Karate.

It is fair to say that discipline within the club or *dojo* is expected to be rigid. Students are expected to conform to the accepted etiquette of the style of Karate they are studying.

After some time students may find that their training in Karate goes beyond that of purely a sport. There are many fighting arts both established and developed in the Western world which are widely known as sports, but few have any philosophical aspect associated with their teachings.

The traditional styles of Karate encompass not only the physical application of techniques, but also a development of the spirit and self realisation through hard and disciplined training methods.

How to join
Visit the various clubs in your area – see what is suitable for you. It should be expected that an instructor will allow you to watch a training session prior to your joining the *dojo*. Be as certain as you can about the credentials of the instructor(s) – remember that there are many less than scrupulous Karate teachers.

Within various countries there are officially recognised bodies to which clubs should be affiliated and of which they may even be members – ask the instructor about this. Enter the *dojo* with your eyes open – find out what the fees are, for both training and for gradings, and whether you are covered by insurance for injury, etc.

It is generally accepted that the novice student will take part in a beginners course for a period of maybe 8–12 weeks. Equipment required during this period will not amount to more than some loose clothing. After this basic introductory course you would be expected to buy a Karate suit (*gi*) and having bought this you would probably not need any further equipment for some time.

Club etiquette and procedure

Karate is a martial art and within the system there is a hierarchy, ranging from the President of the organisation to the novice student.

There are many routines and regulations which must be followed, some of which are particular to a specific style or organisation. Knowing this it would not be appropriate to go into any great detail on the range of procedures.

General club etiquette, relating to *Kyokushin* Karate, is explained here only as a term of reference and cited as an example of what you should possibly expect.

How to wear a Karate *Gi*

The *gi* or karate uniform should be worn as illustrated in the photograph.

Your *gi* must be clean and always kept tidy while being worn, and in general it should be worn left side over right, with the appropriate badges.

How to fold a Karate *Gi*

Folding your *gi* is a discipline in itself – you should take care and be precise in this formality in the same way as you would attempt perfection in your Karate techniques.

Lay your *gi* jacket and trousers on the floor as in Fig. 3a. Place the trousers over the centre, turning up the trouser end (Fig. 3b). Fold one side of the jacket over including folding the sleeve (Fig. 3c) and repeat for the other side (Fig. 3d). Turn up the end of the *gi* jacket (Fig. 3e) and roll up the *gi* (Figs 3f and 3g). To finish off tie your belt around the folded *gi* (Fig. 3h).

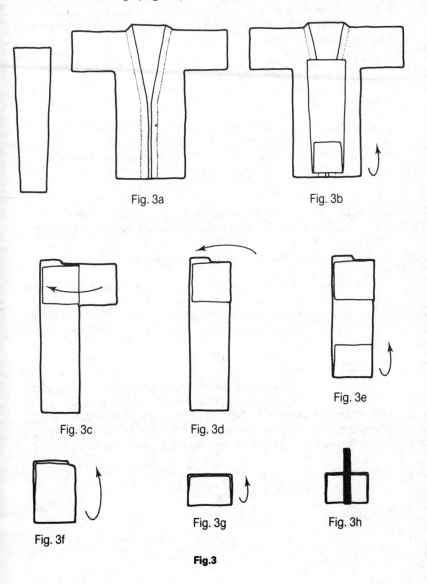

Fig. 3a

Fig. 3b

Fig. 3c

Fig. 3d

Fig. 3e

Fig. 3f

Fig. 3g

Fig. 3h

Fig.3

Dojo etiquette

When entering and leaving a *dojo* the word *Osu* is said loudly and is accompanied by the bow. When a junior member speaks to a senior member (a black belt), once again the procedure of bow and *Osu* is relevant. The correct titles should be used to address your instructors and seniors. These are:

Under black belt – *Kohai*
1st Dan and 2nd Dan – *Senpai*
3rd Dan and 4th Dan – *Sensei*
5th Dan and above – *Shihan*

In all walks of life certain formalities have to be followed; so it is in Karate, where there are many formalities to be followed in order to develop etiquette, respect and, most of all, discipline. Discipline is always heavily emphasised in a *dojo*.

The word *Osu*

The word *Osu* in its basic translation means 'to push' or 'to endure', so the implication is that one will push oneself to the limit of one's ability and endure the consequences. It is also a word which expresses a greeting and replaces words such as: 'yes', 'I will do it' and 'excuse me'.

It has been stated that the word *Osu* is 'of ten thousand meanings expressing the willingness to strive against all odds to persevere on the road to physical, mental and spiritual strength . . . a communication of respect to one's seniors and responsibility to one's juniors'.

The *kiai*

The *kiai* in its basic form is a shout used to emphasise and develop courage, character, power, endurance and breathing. A shout is a very natural expression to the human being. In your Karate training you will slowly begin to understand the *kiai* as a means of developing endurance and spirit whilst performing *kihon*, *kata* and *kumite*.

How to tie a belt

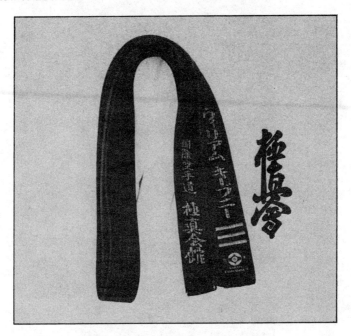

Tying a belt traditionally has to be done correctly and it must feel secure around you.

The procedure should be carried out with confidence and proficiency. You should after a time be able to tie and untie a belt without looking at what you are doing – it will become a reflex.

The eight steps are as follows:

1 Place the belt across your middle (Fig. 4a);
2 Wrap the belt around you so that it crosses over at the back, and bring both ends out in front of you (Fig. 4b);
3 Pass your left end over your right, and tuck it under (Fig. 4c);
4 Prepare the belt (Fig. 4d);
5 Cross your right end over your left (Fig. 4e);
6 Pull your left end through the loop (Fig. 4f);
7 Pull tightly (Fig. 4g);
8 Check that the belt ends are of equal length (Fig. 4h).

Fig.4a

Fig.4b

Fig.4c

Fig.4d

Fig.4e

Fig.4f

Fig.4g

Fig.4h

Gradings

The purpose of having a grading system within any martial art is to gauge the progress of the individual's ability using a grading examination based on a set syllabus.

The grading system is basically in existence as a means of measuring your progress within Karate. Each step or level of learning has to be encountered carefully ensuring that, to the best of your ability, you have understood and reached a level of proficiency acceptable to the grading examiners.

It is a point worth remembering that the colour of a belt does not make the *karateka*, but it is the ability of the person wearing the belt which gives it its worth and acceptability.

10th and 9th *Kyu*	White
8th and 7th *Kyu*	Blue
6th and 5th *Kyu*	Yellow
4th and 3rd *Kyu*	Green
2nd and 1st *Kyu*	Brown
1st Dan and above	Black

The above list of coloured belts is used in the *Kyokushinkai* system of Karate and by some other forms of Karate also. It should be noted that there are styles of Karate which have differing coloured belts for each *kyu* grade. Fundamentally, however, once the *karateka* has reached the Dan Grade level, a black belt is worn.

The bowing procedure

The bowing procedure is a very important part of the etiquette within a *dojo*. In its simplest form it indicates respect, acknowledgement and goodbye. Always remember that your eyes must never look down, but be directed in front of you or at your partner (see Fig. 5).

Fig.5a

Fig.5b

Fig.5c

Fig.5d

The kneeling procedure

The kneeling procedure, as illustrated in Fig. 6 below, is one method utilised in a Karate *dojo*. Ensure that throughout this procedure your eyes are directed forwards. To stand up, simply reverse the illustrated procedure.

Fig.6a

Fig.6b

Fig.6c

Fig.6d

Conditioning exercises

Conditioning in its basic form is a series of exercises which can develop your level of fitness and endurance so that your body can respond to the demands within Karate training, when the need arises. The importance of body conditioning can be related to the tuning of a car engine, in that everything should be able to function correctly. This, of course, is important in Karate training, as is the correct form of breathing. Once the body is conditioned, it can operate effectively to respond to the demands put upon it, such as kicking, blocking and thrusting, and accordingly the mind can work in conjunction to make faster decisions. It is very important to set your body conditioning exercises at the correct level in relation to your ability when you are training – do not attempt to do too much too soon.

Push ups

When doing push ups on your knuckles, palms or fingers (as in Fig. 7), it is essential to concentrate on correct form throughout the whole body during the exercise (i.e. hands, body and legs). When using your knuckles for push ups, ensure that only the first two knuckles (*seiken*) are in contact with the floor and that your fist is held firm – this will automatically ensure a strong wrist. When bringing your body down, so that your nose touches the floor, your fists should still be held firm in the same position as when you began the exercise. Also ensure that your back and legs are straight, not curved, so that your whole body is working. Finally, you must breathe in as you lower your body and breathe out as you push up. You can breathe through your nose or mouth.

This exercise develops the chest and arms as well as benefiting the cardiovascular system.

Important note: Juniors must never attempt push ups on either their knuckles or finger tips. It is advisable that female students practice the push up movement only half way.

Fig.7a

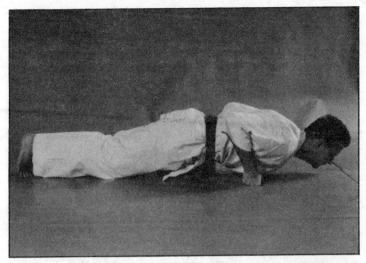

Fig.7b

Fig.7c

Sit ups

There are many ways of doing sit ups which you can see in any gymnasium throughout the world and each has its own merit. Traditionally, whilst practising this exercise in a *dojo*, a student will interlock his or her legs with an assistant. Figure 8 illustrates the isolated sit up, where the knees are bent and the hands are positioned in front. Note that your back and neck should be held straight and firm, and ensure that your back does not fully touch the ground. When pulling up, breathe out, and when lowering, breathe in.

Amongst other things this exercise helps to develop strong stomach muscles.

Fig.8a

Fig.8b

Fig.8c

Squats

It is very important that throughout this exercise your back remains straight (see Fig. 9). As a general rule, it is important to look straight ahead or upwards during the squat. Also, it is not advisable to bend too low – as a guide do not permit your backside to go below your knee level.

During this exercise you can breathe in as you go down and breathe out as you go up.

Fig.9a

Fig.9b

Fig.9c

Stretching

It is important that, each time before you begin your basic Karate training, you perform certain stretching exercises for various parts of the body. The main principle of stretching is to motivate and stimulate the muscles and joints of the body, in order to reduce the possibility of injury.

Four in one exercise

As you will see in Fig. 10, this exercise is geared to strengthening the leg and ankle at the same time as creating elasticity.

On the following pages we illustrate some of the stretching exercises which are also combinations; as well as stretching, this will help your balance and co-ordination and will improve certain kicks that you will learn as you progress. In addition, these exercises can develop your strength and flexibility. Finally, it should be stressed again that it is essential to follow a general stretching routine before any form of Karate training or exercise. Also illustrated are the forward bend (Fig. 11), the seated general stretch (Fig. 12) and the splits (Fig. 13).

Caution should be exercised in performing all stretching exercises and you should begin with care and not overdo the exercises, because this may result in injury.

Fig.10a

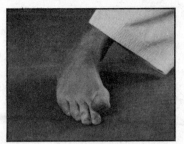

Fig.10b

Fig.10c

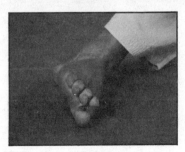

Fig.10d

Fig.10e

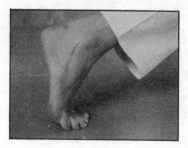

Fig.10f

Fig.10g

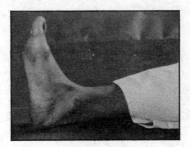

Fig.10h

Fig.11a

Fig.11b

Fig.12a

Fig.12b

Fig.12c

Fig.13a

Fig.13b

Fig.13c

Breathing

In all forms of sports and martial arts it is essential to have and maintain a correct method of breathing in order to maximise your efforts. By breathing correctly and efficiently you can create an increase in overall power in not only Karate but other martial arts and sports.

There are various methods of breathing used in martial arts but we will concentrate on two methods: *Ibuki* breathing and *Nogare* breathing.

Ibuki breathing

In various advanced *katas*, *ibuki* breathing is used. Throughout the *kata* the *ibuki* breathing is performed as explained below – the completion of the last forced breath of the *ibuki* occurs on the completion of the actual technique used (i.e. the block or the punch).

By using the *ibuki* method of breathing you can improve your lung capacity and clean your respiratory system by inhaling clean oxygen, which is in turn circulated within the blood stream. *Ibuki* breathing can also contribute to a hardening of the body, which can take the form of strengthening the stomach and diaphragm. You should note that the diaphragm in the martial arts is an important source of power. In certain circumstances, *ibuki* breathing can also correct irregularities in your breathing pattern, which are brought on by external forces. It is said that if your breathing is controlled, then your emotions can be controlled and that, in addition, *ibuki* breathing can positively develop increased fighting spirit and concentration. If you can master this method of breathing from the lower abdomen, you will have a very good chance of controlling both mental and physical emotions.

Performance of **ibuki**
(a) Inhale quickly and sharply through your nose or mouth taking the air deeply into your lungs.
(b) Harden your abdomen and force out a sharp long breath, with the tip of your tongue pushing behind your lower teeth. The remainder of your tongue should fall naturally back to your throat. Your throat should be kept wide open and you should harden all the muscles of your body, in particular your abdomen.
(c) Your chest should maintain expansion throughout while the air is forced out for a mental count of five by the stomach's contraction from deep down in the region of the lower abdomen. The noise of the *ibuki* should not vary in force or pitch but remain constant from start to finish.
(d) When the *ibuki* is nearly complete you should force out a strong last breath which should harden the abdomen; this last breath must be very strong and should expel all air. This completes the *ibuki* breathing method.

Nogare **breathing**
Nogare breathing is simply a method of controlling and calming your breathing pattern after strenuous activity. It can also be used to control your breathing during actual combat, in order to give no indication to your opponent of your breathing condition.

Performance of **nogare**
(a) Inhale gently through your nose or mouth into your lungs and exhale gently, holding your stomach muscles tight.
(b) Control the noise of your breathing on the exhaling action by placing your tongue firmly against the upper palate of your mouth, with the tip of your tongue pushed lightly against a slight gap formed between your teeth. It is again important to maintain chest expansion throughout this exercise.

3

Stances

The most common stances are:
- Heisoku Dachi
- Musubi Dachi
- Heiko Dachi
- Uchi Hachi Ji Dachi
- Fudo Dachi
- Zenkutsu Dachi
- Sanchin Dachi

- Tsuru Ashi Dachi
- Moro Ashi Dachi
- Kake Dachi
- Neko Ashi Dachi
- Kiba Dachi
- Kokutsu Dachi

The basics of the stance

In Karate it is of primary importance to learn the fundamental aspects of a correct stance. The student beginning Karate should be receptive to new experiences and in essence learn, like a child, how to stand properly. The Karate student must at all times remain in control of his or her body, retaining balance whether attacking or defending against an opponent. Taking this further, the student should be able to convert a successful defence into a successful counter-attack and must be able to use the most logical stance for the technique. The student should also take into consideration the nature of the attack and select a stance that best suits it.

It should be remembered that once the student has a proficient ability in balance and co-ordination, speed is of vital importance –

the student must therefore be fully aware of where to position his or her centre of gravity. When possible, the upper half of the body in all stances, whether attacking or defensive, must be perpendicular to the floor.

Once the student has successfully understood the principles of the basic Karate stance, it will follow that he or she will be able to develop his or her own natural fighting position and stance for practice sparring in the *dojo*. It is important to remember that there is no single correct stance – the stance differs from style to style. It is important never to confuse the two principles of:

(a)   The basic Karate stances for practising techniques; and
(b)   The fighting stance.

A good fighting stance enables you to attack, defend and counter-attack efficiently, with the minimum of movement at maximum speed.

As a general rule, a fighting stance should be as follows:

(i)   Your feet should be approximately a shoulder width apart and a shoulder width in length. Your body weight should be approximately split half and half on each leg.
(ii)   Your hands are held in a relaxed position at approximately shoulder or chin height with your elbows close to your ribs, guarding your body.

It may take many years to develop a good fighting stance, so you should analyse and experiment with various stances until you arrive at what works for you. Remember that correct and effective attacks depend on the ability to transfer your body weight forwards, backwards and sideways. It is not the purpose of this book to teach advanced forms of fighting, so we have only briefly touched on the student's fighting stance. We have however concentrated on the basic traditional Karate stances which, like all aspects of Karate, must be practised diligently and endlessly if you are to succeed in maximising your potential.

The learning process and development of the stances used in Karate can generally be divided into the following elements:

(a)   Discipline;
(b)   Correct posture;
(c)   Isometrics;
(d)   A combination of discipline, correct posture and isometrics.

(a) Discipline

Discipline can be seen as the ability to hold the stance in the correct position for a given period of time.

(b) Correct posture

This can be described as the ability to take the correct position which the stance demands, in terms of position, balance and weight distribution. It should be noted that all stances have a 'forward lean' of approximately 1° from the body's natural vertical line, that the back should be erect and that the feet should grip the floor in traction.

(c) Isometrics of stances

This is the exercise involved in strengthening the whole body in order to increase the development, power and performance of the stance.

(d) A combination of discipline, posture and isometrics

It is important to note that to obtain full benefit in the execution of the stance, discipline, posture and isometrics must be moulded together and performed in one movement.

Heisoku Dachi

Place your feet together and point your toes straight ahead and distribute your body weight equally on both feet as in Fig. 14.

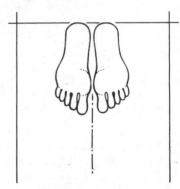

Fig.14 Heisoku Dachi

This stance can be used for meditation.

It is a natural body position – your knees should be slightly bent and your whole body should be pulled firm.

Musubi Dachi
Your heels should be placed together with your feet pointing approximately at a 45° angle, and your weight distributed equally on both feet. This position is a good stance to be used in meditation.

Again, it is a natural body position – your knees should be slightly bent and your whole body should be pulled firm.

It is the first and last step of many of the advanced formal exercises (*kata*).

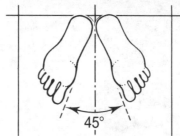

Fig.15 Musubi Dachi

Heiko Dachi
Position your feet approximately one shoulder width apart, with your toes straight ahead (i.e. parallel) and your body weight distributed equally on both feet.

Your knees should be slightly bent and your whole body pulled in isometrics.

It is a ready stance (*yoi dachi*) which keeps the body alert and prepared for attacks. It is also a position from which one moves into formal exercises (*kata*).

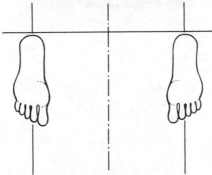

Fig.16 Heiko Dachi

Uchi Hachi Ji Dachi

With your feet positioned approximately one shoulder width apart, pivot on the balls of your feet moving the heels of your feet out and pointing your toes in slightly, with your body weight distributed equally on both feet. Your knees should be slightly bent.

You can exercise the isometric pull, once the stance has been attained, by pulling your feet, with the emphasis on your heels, to a central direction inwards without them moving.

This stance develops the muscles of the lower half of the body, and is generally a movement used in formal exercises (*kata*).

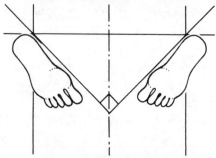

Fig.17 Uchi Hachi Ji Dachi

Fudo Dachi

Your feet should be positioned approximately one shoulder width apart with your toes pointing slightly outwards. Your knees should be slightly bent, with your body weight distributed equally on both feet.

The isometric pull, once the stance has been attained, can be exercised by pulling from the heels of both feet to a central direction inwards without moving them.

This stance is generally used for exchanging formal bows and when awaiting commands.

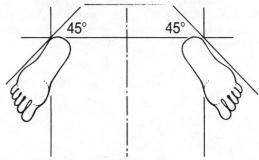

Fig.18 Fudo Dachi

Zenkutsu Dachi

Your feet should be positioned approximately one shoulder width apart and two shoulder widths and half a foot in front of each other. Put your front foot straight ahead and bend your knee, so that it is positioned vertically over the centre of your front foot. Your back leg should be straight with your foot angled outwards slightly, at approximately 45°.

Your body weight should be distributed approximately 60% on your front foot and 40% on your back foot.

Once the stance has been attained, the isometric pull can be exercised as follows:

Imagine both feet on two parallel lines, your rear foot being pulled forwards by a spring and your front foot being pulled backwards.

This stance is used mainly for front kicks and punches because the power is exerted from the rear of your hips and thighs for middle thrusts and blocking techniques. In its basic form it can be used for pre-arranged fighting (i.e. *ippon*, *sanbon* and *yakusoku kumite*). In advanced movements or freestyle fighting stances, this stance is shortened by at least 30cm but still retains the same principles.

Movement in this stance:
Turn on the ball of your front foot so that the heel moves inwardly at approximately 45°. Your back foot should then move forward on a straight line and as you move forwards with your back leg, your body will stay at the same hip and shoulder level. Whilst moving forward it is important also to ensure that the 1° 'forward lean' is maintained. Both legs work together, your front leg pulling backwards and your back pulling forwards, thus generating speed and strengthening the stance.

It must be noted that in all direct frontal attacks in *Zenkutsu Dachi*, your hips and shoulders are square and when executing blocks and some roundhouse strikes, there is an approximate angle of 45° on both hips and shoulders.

Fig.19 Zenkutsu Dachi

Kokutsu Dachi

Place one leg in front of the other so that the distance from your front foot to your rear foot is approximately three 'feet' (i.e. your own foot measurement) taken from your back heel. The gauge between the front and back foot (i.e. width) is approximately 5cm. Your rear foot is positioned at 45° and the heel of your front foot is raised approximately 5cm, with the weight taken on the ball of your foot and all toes equally in contact with the ground. Your front foot should be pointing straight ahead with your knee bent so that your knee is positioned vertically over the centre of your front foot. Your body should sink into a position as if you were sitting in a chair, in order to create a bend in both knees. It is essential that your back leg should not be bent too much nor your hips lowered too far. Your whole body should be in a strong and comfortable position to enable you to execute movements correctly. Your body weight should be distributed with approximately 60% on your back foot and 40% on your front foot.

The isometric pull in the stance is similar to *Zenkutsu Dachi*, where the rear foot is pulled forward and the front foot pulled back (see *Zenkutsu Dachi* stance on page 50).

This stance is very mobile allowing kicks from both legs and can be used and adapted in fighting.

Movement in this stance:
Turn your front foot inwards at 45°, taking your weight on the ball of your foot and simultaneously placing your whole foot on the ground. Move through with your back leg on a straight line to the position explained above, so that your front foot is pointing in front and your rear foot is angled at 45°. It should be noted that in *Kokutsu Dachi*, only your hip and shoulder angle changes when you are executing blocks or strikes. Most blocks and roundhouse strikes have an angle of 45° on the hips and shoulders and, in all direct frontal attacks, your hip position should be square.

Fig.20 Kokutsu Dachi

Sanchin Dachi

Place your feet approximately one shoulder width apart. The heel of
your front foot should be positioned so that it lies approximately
5cm in front of the toes of your back foot, with your body weight
distributed equally on both feet. Your feet should be positioned so
that your toes point inwards to give an angle and your knees bend
correctly. To obtain the correct angle, place both hands in the
morote tsuki (double punch) position directly in front of the body at
chudan level – use an imaginary plumb line from the front and
centre of your fists and observe where this line would drop onto the
floor. An imaginary line drawn on the outside of both feet should
apex on the point where the plumb line would drop (see Fig. 21).

The isometric pull once the stance has been attained can be
exercised as follows. With your buttocks pulled up, the heels of your
feet should be pulled in a circular direction to the imaginary centre
of gravity of your entire body, projected between your feet. It is
important that you bend your knees and that they point towards the
apex of the triangle (i.e. they will be at a similar angle as your feet).
Maximum torque of the lower part of the body is essential. Under
no circumstances should the torque be applied in such a way as to
produce a shaking movement in the legs. The upper body torque is
generated through chest, shoulder and arm movement.

This stance gives you a strong balanced position, and strengthens
your whole body. It enables quick movements and changes of
direction and is used for performing punches, blocks, kicks and
blocking with the legs.

The *Sanchin* stance itself is made up of a combination of triangles
which contribute to the overall strength and development of the
stance.

Movement in this stance:

Without changing the angles made by your feet and knees, move
your back foot forwards in a semi-circular motion and assume the
correct position as described above.

Fig.21 Sanchin Dachi

Tsuru Ashi Dachi

Raise one foot up approximately knee height and pull your big toe upwards and your small toes downwards; the knee and thigh of your raised leg should be parallel to the ground. Your other foot should be angled at approximately 45° and should be slightly bent.

Once the stance has been achieved, isometric pull can be exercised by pulling the whole body firm.

Movement in this stance:
Movement in this stance is normally combined and co-ordinated with the majority of moving stances.

This stance is used to control balance on one leg, which will enable you to perfect various kicks.

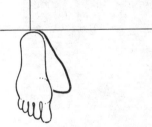

Fig.22 Tsuru Ashi Dachi

Moro Ashi Dachi

Place your feet approximately one shoulder width apart, and then position one foot approximately 5cm in front of the other – ensure that both feet are parallel, and that your knees are slightly bent.

Your body weight should be distributed equally on both feet.

Once the stance has been achieved, the isometric pull can be exercised as follows. With your buttocks pulled up, pull your front foot backwards and your back foot forwards without actually moving your feet, with both knees pushed slightly outwards.

This stance is quick and mobile and can be used for all attacks and defences (e.g. kicks, punches, strikes and blocks).

Movement in this stance:
Move your back leg forwards in a straight line by approximately one shoulder width and, with your feet one shoulder width apart, move your left leg forward slightly so that it lies approximately 5cm behind your right heel. NB You should lead into the stance with the ball of your foot and not the heel.

This stance is very mobile, allowing jump kicks and normal kicks from both legs and it can be used and adapted in fighting.

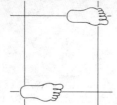

Fig.23 Moro Ashi Dachi

Kake Dachi
Hook your left foot behind your right foot, ensuring that your right foot is at a right angle and that your left foot is supported on the ball of the foot with the heel raised high. Your left knee should be positioned tightly behind your right knee, and both knees must be

slightly bent. The weight distribution should be approximately 90% on one foot and 10% on the other.

The isometric pull in this stance can be exercised by pulling both knees together and twisting your hips in the direction of your intended forward movement. It is important also to ensure that both knees remain slightly bent.

Movement in this stance:
This is usually performed at right angles to the direction in which your body is pointing. Movement in this stance is always performed by jumping and landing on your right foot; your right leg should jump approximately one shoulder width's distance and your left leg should simultaneously move in the same direction to the rear of your right leg, in order to support the stance.

Fig.24 Kake Dachi

Neko Ashi Dachi

Place one leg in front of the other so that the distance from your front foot to your back foot is approximately two 'feet' (i.e. twice your own foot measurement), as measured from the heel of your back foot. The distance between front and back foot (i.e. the width of the stance) is approximately 5cm. Your back foot needs to be positioned at 45° and the heel of your front foot should be raised as high as possible, thus taking the weight on the ball of your foot and keeping all your toes equally in contact with the ground. You should point your front foot straight ahead with your knees bent, so that your knee is vertically over the centre of the ball of your foot. Your body must now sink low to create a bend in both knees which should be slightly lower than in *Kokutsu Dachi*. The body weight distribution should be approximately 90% on your back foot and 10% on your front foot.

The isometric pull in the stance is similar to *Kokutsu Dachi* as described on pages 51–2. Again, it must be emphasised that your back leg should not be bent too much nor your hips too low. Your body should be in a strong and comfortable position so that you are able to execute movements correctly.

The stance is very mobile allowing you to kick with both legs and it can be used and adapted in fighting.

Fig.25 Neko Ashi Dachi

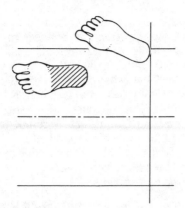

Movement in this stance:
The movement in this stance is similar to that described in the section on *Kokutsu Dachi* (see p. 52).

Kiba Dachi
Place your legs approximately two shoulder widths apart, ensuring that both feet are pointing straight ahead and are parallel. Bend both knees and lower your hips to a position as illustrated in Figure 26. Your weight should be distributed equally on both feet.

The isometric pull once the stance has been achieved can be exercised as follows: Push your knees outwards, pull your feet towards your centre line and pull your buttocks up.

Movement in this stance:
In this stance there are various forward, angled and straight methods of movement.

Examples of movement:

(a)   It is possible to move forwards at 45° in a straight line – your front heel should be turned so that your foot points at 45°. Your back foot needs to move forwards in a straight line before you put the ball of your foot down. With your foot pointing straight ahead and your heel turned outwards at 45°, you can assume the *Kiba Dachi* stance.

(b)   You can move at 45° in a circular movement with your front heel turned so that your foot also points at 45°. Your back foot should slide in a semicircular movement to the front foot and then move directly into *Kiba Dachi* at 45°, again in a semicircular movement.

(c) It is also possible to move forwards in a direct straight line. To do so, pivot from the *Kiba Dachi* stance on the ball of your right (i.e. front) foot, so that your foot points in a straight line. At the same time, pivot on the ball of your left (i.e. back) foot and raise the heel (this will help you to remain balanced). Slide through with your left foot in a straight line, putting your foot straight ahead and, at the same time, raise your right heel. Pivot on both feet into *Kiba Dachi* to complete the movement.

(d) Alternatively, move in a direct straight line. To do so, move your left (i.e. back) leg in front or behind your right leg with a small step and then move your right leg across into *Kiba Dachi* to complete the movement.

This stance is very good for developing your legs and generating power in your hips and back; it also strengthens the diaphragm.

Fig.26 Kiba Dachi

4

Blocks

The most common blocks are:
- Jodan Uke
- Mae Gedan Barai
- Chudan Soto Uke
- Chudan Uchi Uke

About the block

It is sometimes said that the first technique used by a *karateka* in a real situation is the block. This is because Karate is fundamentally used as self-defence and the *karateka* is not generally the aggressor or the instigator of an incident.

It is also true in Karate that the block and attack are one, since the execution of a block leads directly to a counter-attack; in essence a perfectly executed block makes for an effective attack.

The practice of blocking is extremely important as is the correct use of the block. It is important to remember that it is not a good idea to stop your opponent's attack dead, but that it is useful to try to parry it away. By way of illustration, imagine a direct attack from above descending on your head. If you block the attack with your arm at right angles to the direction of the attack, your arm will absorb the whole force of the attack (Fig. 27). This could be disastrous if your attacker is using, for example, an iron bar or a heavy object. However, if you block the attack at an angle, so that the descending force is deflected to some extent as in Figure 28 the block will obviously be more effective.

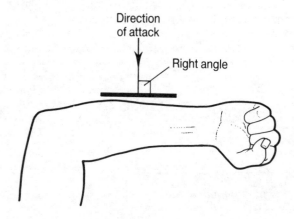

Fig.27 Blocking at a right angle

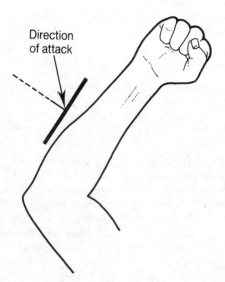

Fig.28 Deflecting an attack

The blocking technique

Care must be taken when practising blocks in order to avoid undue injury. Timing is an essential feature of the block, and indeed of all Karate techniques, so it is important to practise regularly. The development of your blocking techniques is fundamentally important, as the block is generally accepted as the first step in a counter-attack. As your Karate training develops, you will see that blocking techniques can be transformed into other sorts of weapons – for example, they have various self-defence applications.

Only a few blocking methods from the vast number in Karate are explained here but the method of execution illustrated is the basic, theoretical method of performing the block. In actual combat, the process of blocking in relation to the basic technique is somewhat different in its application.

Jodan Uke – the upper block

This block is used to deflect an attack to the head or face.

The block starts with your left arm raised above your head (as in

Fig.29   **Fig.30**

Fig.31

Fig.32

Fig.33

Fig.34

Fig. 29). Now bring your elbow down to the centre of your body in a vertical position, (as in Fig. 30), and cross your blocking arm (the right) in front of your body (Fig. 31).

Move it through into the upper block position, blocking with your forearm and turning or thrusting your arm into the finishing position (Figs 32 and 33).

Mae Gedan Barai – the lower block

This block is generally used to deflect attacks which are directed at the groin or middle.

From the starting position, with your right arm by your side (as in Fig. 35), execute the block by bringing your left hand in line with your right ear (Fig. 36) ensuring that your right arm, which is protecting your groin, is on a centre line. Now drive your left hand down into the block from the ear position, block the oncoming attack with your forearm and, in doing so, turn or thrust your arm into the final position (Fig. 37).

Fig.35

Fig.36

Fig.37

Fig.38

Chudan Soto Uke – the middle outside block

This block is used to deflect attacks to the middle level of the body.

The fist of your covering (left) arm comes up to your shoulder in front of your body and parallel to the ground and your blocking (right) arm is placed behind your head, approximately one fist's distance away from your head (Fig. 39). Moving in a semicircle, execute the block with the back of your right forearm, twisting into the final position at the end of the movement, just past the centre line of your body, with your fist just below your jaw line and your shoulders slightly angled (Fig. 40). At the same time, remember to return your other hand to the 'ready punch' position. The blocking arm must be held very firm and the shoulders angled (Fig. 41).

Fig.39

Fig.40

Fig.41

Chudan Uchi Uke – the middle inside block

Like *Chudan Soto Uke*, this technique is used to deflect an attack to the middle level.

It is important to remember that your blocking (right) arm comes from under your left arm (Fig. 42) and that your left arm must be in a straight horizontal line in front of your body. Your blocking arm passes across your body over your left arm (as in Fig. 43), thus executing the block with your forearm and twisting to the finished position slightly past the line of your right shoulder, with your fist just below the line of your jaw. At the same time, remember to return your left hand to the ready punch position. Your blocking arm must be held very strong and your shoulders should be angled (Fig. 44).

There are many other blocks which the student will learn once he or she has mastered the principles set out in the four blocks described in this chapter.

The following are some more complicated blocks which the student will eventually encounter: *Juji Uke* and *Shotei Uke*.

Fig.42

Fig.43

Fig.44

Fig.45

Fig.46

Fig.47

Fig.48

Fig.49

Fig.50

5

Punching and Striking

- Punching and striking techniques
- How to form a fist
- Strikes and punches
- Different techniques
- Hand conditioning and breaking techniques

Punching and striking techniques

There are many striking techniques used in Karate, but it is common sense that only certain techniques will be effective in certain circumstances. Experience and correct tuition within a *dojo* will give you the knowledge necessary to maximise their effectiveness and to choose the correct technique at the correct time.

Constant practice is one of the main elements that will ensure success. The point to which you should give particular attention is the correct positioning of your hand technique, be it a knife hand strike (*shuto*), an elbow strike (*hijiate*) or whatever – you must learn to maintain the correct principles of forming the technique. For example, it would not be a good idea to punch an oppor.ent with your fist held loosely and your wrist bent, since probably the only damage you would do would be to yourself. This chapter does not give detailed instructions on the various methods of executing strikes because of their sheer number, and, indeed, it also only makes a passing reference to where the attacks may be directed.

In practising these techniques either alone or with a partner, you are advised to take care in order not to cause injury to both yourself and your partner.

How to form a fist

The fist is one of the most important and most frequently used Karate weapons. It is important to note that in executing a punch or strike with your fist, your hand must be held firm. To form a fist, first fold your four fingers tightly as shown, bend the knuckle and clamp your thumb on top of the bent fingers (as shown in Fig. 51). When punching or striking not only should your fist be held firm and your thumb tucked in, but your little finger must also be tucked in tightly.

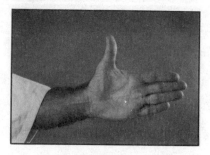

Fig.51a

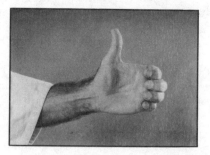

Fig.51b

Fig.51c

Fig.51d

Fig.52a

Fig.52b

Strikes and punches

One important factor in generating power in punching is the way that you form your fist. The power generated depends on how you clench your hand, on the correct distribution of power and on focus. In early practice in a *dojo*, you will perform all punches in the basic stances (e.g. *Fudo Dachi* and *Zenkutsu Dachi*) and it is important to remember a few points which will give you a good background so that you may develop your technique:

  (i)   Begin the practice punching sequence with your left fist at target height and your right fist pulled back to your side as shown (Fig. 53).
 (ii)   Slowly punch with your right hand at the target level and, as you do so, twist your fist at the last moment and simultaneously withdraw your left fist to the left side, twisting your wrist so that the back of your hand ends up pointing towards the ground (Figs 54 and 55).
(iii)   Practise at first using one hand at a time, then use alternatively left, right, etc. As you make progress you can practise a series of different sequences.

Fig.53

Fig.54

Fig.55

Generally, all the striking and blocking techniques can be practised with this basic method, using alternate hands or arms in *Fudo Dachi*. Once you are confident of your ability to execute the technique, you can experiment using various other stances (e.g. *Zenkutsu Dachi*, *Sanchin Dachi*, etc.).

The next level would be to choose a stance, for example *Zenkutsu Dachi*, and a technique, say *Seiken Jodan Tsuki*, and combine the two.

From a left *Zenkutsu Dachi* stance, move forwards into a right *Zenkutsu Dachi* and strike *Seiken Chudan Tsuki* – do this twice using alternate legs and fists. After the third movement, turn 180° and repeat the sequence until you are back where you began (Figure 56).

This practice routine can be used in almost all stances described in chapter 3, by making use of all the various strikes, blocks and kicks illustrated.

Initially, it is essential that this practice is taken slowly, with the emphasis on technique and focus, before thoughts of increasing the speed of execution are entertained.

It should be emphasised that when performing the basic punching techniques as illustrated, your shoulders should be square. This enables you to control your body movement from an early stage. In a fighting situation, you inevitably need to use full power and, consequently, make use of your hip and shoulder to generate maximum power in your punch.

There must be a natural slight bend in your arm when extended, and the focus of your punching fist should be on your centre line. In addition, your wrist should be straight on a horizontal plane.

When punching, the area of your fist which you employ is the *seiken* (that is, the first two knuckles).

At the moment of final impact, you should imagine that you are squeezing a sponge dry of water, which will strengthen your wrist. In addition, at the moment of impact, your whole body should be held firm and your arm and fist should twist as illustrated, just prior to impact.

Fig.56a

Fig.56b

Fig.56c

Fig.56d

Different techniques

Whilst sparring in the *dojo*, it is a good idea to use and hold the *seiken* position at all times, in order to avoid injury to your hands, should you attempt to block an attack with an open hand technique.

Seiken Tsuki – the forefist thrust

Of all the hand techniques in Karate, the *Seiken Tsuki* is arguably the most effective. There are several variations on this technique some of which are illustrated below.

Seiken Jodan Tsuki

The punch is directed to the face with a thrusting action, as in Figure 57.

Fig.57

Seiken Chudan Tsuki

The punch is directed to the middle body (e.g. the solar plexus), again with a thrusting action, as in Figure 58.

Fig.58

Seiken Gedan Tsuki

The punch is directed to the lower body (e.g. the groin) in the same way as those above.

Seiken Ago Uchi

Again the punch is directed to the face, but using a jabbing action and not a thrust, as in Figure 59.

Fig.59

Tettsui – the hammer fist

Your fist should be held as in the *Seiken Tsuki* position, but the striking area is now the base of your fist.

Target areas include the head and body.

Fig.60

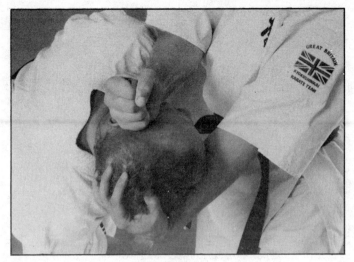

Fig.61

Uraken – the back fist
Again the fist position is similar to the *Seiken Tsuki* and the striking area is the *Seiken*. This technique can be used in a variety of ways, for example downwards, outwards or upwards as in Figure 62, in a thrusting movement to the face (Fig. 63).

Fig.62

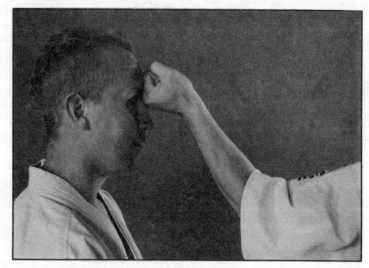

Fig.63

Shuto – the knife hand

This technique can be very effective, but will fail unless your hand is held correctly, with your thumb tucked in and your remaining fingers pressed together and bent slightly (Fig. 64). This is a very adaptable technique and can be targeted to the head or body (as in Figs. 65 and 66).

Fig.64

Fig.65a

Fig.65b

Fig.66a

Fig.66b

Shotei – the heel of the hand
In this open hand technique, your thumb should be tucked in and
your fingers slightly bent to give strength to your hand. Target areas
are the face, body and groin (as in Figures 67 and 68).

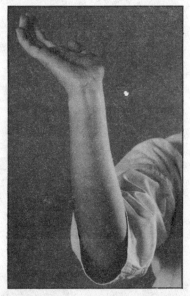

Fig.67

Fig.68

Hiraken – the flat fist

This technique can be used in two ways; with your inner palm (Fig. 69a) or with the base of your bent knuckles (Fig. 69b). In the first method, the target area is generally the ear, in the second the area can be under the nose, the throat or the solar plexus.

Fig.69a **Fig.69b**

Fig.70

Hiji – the elbow
This is the most powerful of all arm techniques but, because of its
very nature, the range of the elbow is restricted to close attack. It
can be used upwards, downwards, behind or in a circular attack to
the head and body.

Fig.71a

Fig.71b

Keiko – the chicken beak

This technique is formed by bringing your five fingers together as illustrated and tensing your finger tips – the target areas can be the face or body.

Fig.72

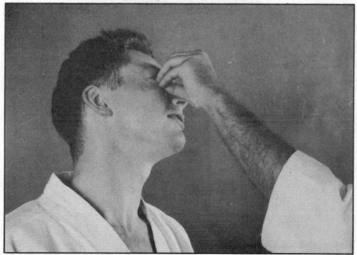

Fig.73

Haito – the inner knife hand

The hand position is similar to the *Shuto* position except that the
striking area is the inner edge of your hand (see Fig. 74).

The target areas are the head, body and groin (Fig. 75).

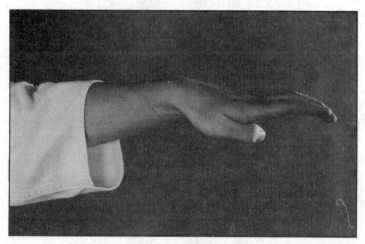

Fig.74

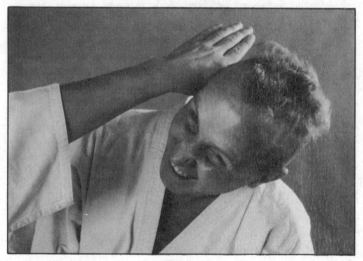

Fig.75

Nukite – the spear hand
Once again this technique is formed in a similar way to the *Shuto*,
except that the striking area is your finger tips as in Figure 76. The
target areas are generally the eyes, the throat and the solar plexus
(Fig. 77).

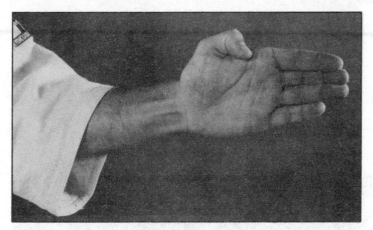

Fig.76

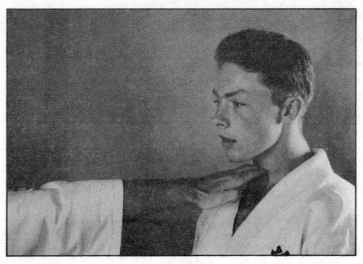

Fig.77

Ippon ken – one finger

In the first example *Oya-Yubi-Kau* (Fig. 78) the thumb knuckle is used for the attack in a position similar to the *Seiken*. In the second example *Naka-Yubi-Ippon-Ken* (Fig. 79) the middle knuckle is extended to provide a strong technique. The target areas can be the face and body.

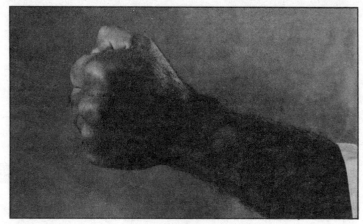

Fig.78

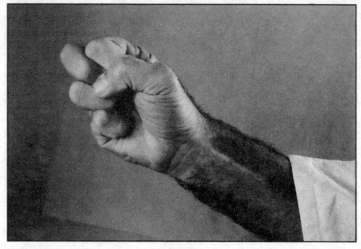

Fig.79

Toho – the sword peak hand

This technique is targeted at the throat using the open hand area from the tip of your thumb to the tip of your index finger – after the initial strike you can squeeze your opponent's windpipe using your thumb and index finger as in Figure 81.

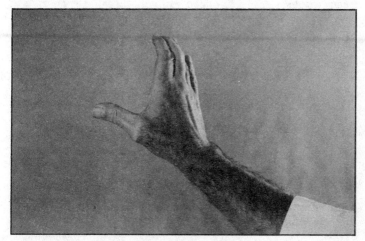

Fig.80

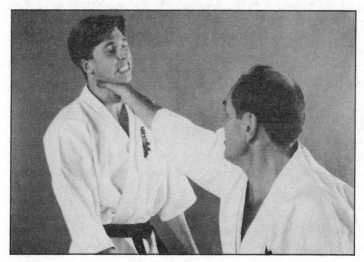

Fig.81

Hand conditioning and breaking (*tameshiwari*) techniques

Conditioning is the process whereby the *Karateka* toughens various parts of the body. For example, in order to give protection to the *Seiken* (forefist), some *Karateka* build up the calluses on their first two knuckles. This can be done in a variety of ways, one of which is by punching repeatedly at a *Makiwara* (a straw or leather punching pad).

The beginner would not be advised to think about conditioning his or her hands at this early stage. This is especially important for junior Karate students under the age of 16.

There are many contrasting opinions regarding the conditioning of your hands and so it is unnecessary and inadvisable for the beginner to attempt to do so without proper guidance and instruction. Injury and permanent damage could be suffered should the inexperienced student wrecklessly attempt to condition his or her hands without supervision.

Also, extreme caution and care are needed for any experienced Karate student, let alone the novice, to attempt to break (*tameshiwari*) any objects as a test of their skills.

Throughout the martial arts world there are many accomplished *Karateka* who have broken a variety of items. None more famous than Masutatsu Oyama whose *tameshiwari* record is legendary.

The breaking of various objects (for example bricks, tiles, etc.) can be a measure of your technique and strength as well as a test of your courage.

Tameshiwari is a very advanced technique which you will encounter later in your Karate career and which, at the moment, should not be attempted.

6

Kicking Techniques

Kicking techniques

It goes without saying that your legs are stronger and more powerful than your arms and that they are effective from a greater distance than your arms when you are punching. When kicking, factors such as balance and co-ordination play a large role in the efficient execution of each technique.

When executing a kick, it is essential that, where possible, you should slightly bend the knee of your supporting leg. You should then use the spring action and, in some instances, a twisting or circular motion. At the point of impact, tense the part of your foot which is coming into contact with the target.

When kicking it is important to use your whole body to generate power and to concentrate on the position of your body and your other leg when striking and not just on your kicking leg.

Finally, you should be conscious of the fact that the techniques illustrated in many instances make use of muscles not normally stressed in everyday life. In order to avoid serious injuries like tears, sprains, etc. you must limber up, warming your muscles with stretching and other exercises.

Using your leg and foot

There are several parts of your leg and foot which can be used as weapons:

Hiza – the knee

The knee can be used in certain circumstances against your opponents face, groin, ribs or legs (see Fig. 82).

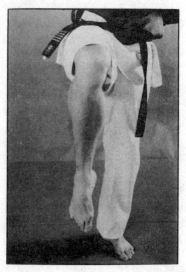

Fig.82a

Fig.82b

Haisoku – the instep

The instep can be used to attack the groin, stomach, face, or neck. When striking with the instep you must ensure that your toes are held together (see Fig. 83).

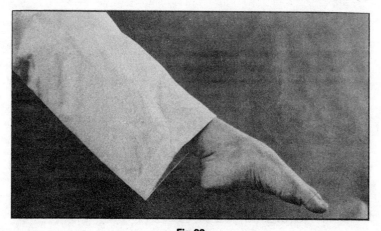

Fig.83

Kakato – the heel

The heel is generally used on an opponent who has fallen or in *ushiro geri* (the back kick) (see Fig. 84).

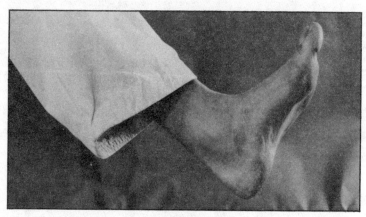

Fig.84

Chusoku – the ball of your foot

This is effective in kicking an opponent to the stomach, face or in using *mawashi geri* (the roundhouse kick) to the ribs and head (see Fig. 85).

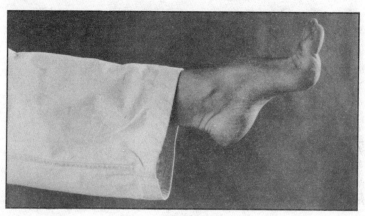

Fig.85

Sokuto – the knife foot

This part of the foot is used in *yoko geri* (the side kick). The target areas can be the stomach, face, knee or hip joint (see Fig. 86).

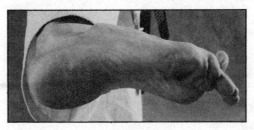

Fig.86

Sune – shin

This area of the leg can be used to attack the thighs, stomach, ribs or indeed the head (see Fig. 87).

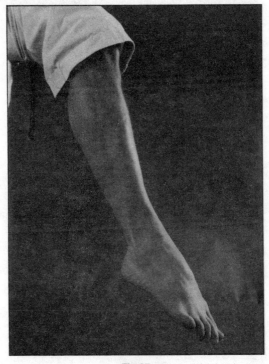

Fig.87

The above are the various parts of the leg or foot which can be used – the following are some of the many kicking techniques which can be used.

The kicks

Hiza Ganmen Geri – the knee kick to the face

This is a very powerful kick and is very effective when fighting close with your opponent. When practising this kick, raise your left knee as high as possible to your left shoulder, ensuring that your toes are pointing downwards (see Fig. 88).

This kick can be used to, amongst others, the groin, solar plexus and head.

Fig.88a

Fig.88b

Kin Geri – the groin kick
Raise your kicking leg as Figure 89. The kick is directed in a straight
line with great speed to the groin area, using the instep. Make sure
that your toes are pointed and return your kicking leg to the original
position, when the kick is complete.

Fig.89a

Fig.89b

Mae Geri – the front kick

This kick begins in a similar way to *kin geri* with the kicking leg being raised as illustrated in Figure 90a, and then driven or thrust out towards either the stomach or face, Figures 90b and 90c. It is important to pull the toes of your kicking foot back and to strike using the *chusoku* (the ball of your foot).

Fig.90a

Fig.90b

Fig.90c

Kansetsu Geri – the joint kick

This kick is generally targeted at the knee joint using the *sokuto* (the side of the foot). It is essential that the leg which you use for the attack is brought up directly to the centre of your body with your knee bent as illustrated in Figure 91b. The attack is then delivered away from the body in an outwards and downwards thrust to the

Fig.91a

knee joint (Fig. 91c). After impact, you should immediately return your kicking leg to the starting position along the reverse of its original route.

Fig.91b

Fig.91c

Yoko Geri – the side kick
This kick is very similar to *kansetsu geri* except that the target area
can be either the midrift (for example, the stomach or ribs) or the
face. Bring your attacking leg up to the centre of your body, and
raise your knee as high as possible, before thrusting the kick to the
side. Remember to keep your big toe pulled back and up, thus
striking with the *sokuto* part of your foot. Now return your leg to its
original position immediately after the attack. See Fig. 92.

Fig.92a

Fig.92b

Fig.92c

Mawashi Geri – the roundhouse kick

Bend your kicking leg and raise it to the side of your body, ensuring that you maintain good balance with your supporting leg, as in Figure 93. Thrust your kicking foot round, keeping your knee high, and also bring your knee round on the same plane. Finally, straighten your whole leg on impact. You must twist your hips into the kick and you can use either the *haisoku* (the instep) or *chusoku* (the ball of the foot) in executing this kick.

Fig.93a

Fig.93b

Fig.93c

Ushiro Geri – the back kick
This kick is used against an opponent who is behind you and you will
be aiming at the groin, stomach or face. Raise your attacking leg as
in Figure 94, with your knee uppermost, then snap or thrust your leg
out using the heel to make contact with your opponent. Balance is
essential and you may have to lean slightly forwards with the upper
part of your body in order to maintain it.

Fig.94a

Fig.94b

Conclusion

Although there are many other kicks used in Karate, the basic forms of kicking illustrated in this chapter will provide a good foundation for the development of the advanced kicking techniques. As with all Karate techniques, it is vital that kicking is practised regularly and with care.

7

Fighting and Sparring

- Counter techniques
- Sanbon Kumite – three step sparring
- Free-style fighting

Counter techniques

Basic formal practice fighting

Obviously, simply to learn all the previous techniques in this book and to practise them in isolation would not be of much use in a real situation.

In order to develop the techniques you should always, at some stage in your training régime, practise them separately. However, in addition to this it is essential that the techniques you have learnt should be put into practice with the help of a training partner. It should be stressed that, in all practice, care must always be taken at all times in order to minimalise the chances of any unnecessary injury.

Practice fighting can take various forms – for example, there is the situation where attacks and blocks are a series of predetermined set techniques or there is free-style practice fighting, which is literally the freedom to use any techniques. This is effectively a match between two opponents. It is extremely important that the beginner should begin with predetermined techniques. This type of practice **can take either one step or three step forms (either in a stationary** position or moving). In the more common three step system, the attacker attacks with three techniques and the defender blocks three times before counter-attacking at the end of the routine.

A correct focus of techniques is essential and it is a good idea not to practise them too quickly at first – concentrate on correct form rather than speed.

Illustrated below is an example of **three step sparring** which can be used as a guide to follow.

Sanbon Kumite – three step sparring

Both opponents **L** and **R** stand in *fudo dachi* (Fig. 95).

R moves back into right *zenkutsu dachi* and blocks right *mae gedan barai* (Fig. 96).

R moves forward into left *zenkutsu dachi* and strikes with left *jodan tsuki*. Simultaneously **L** moves into right *zenkutsu dachi* and blocks with right *jodan uke* (Fig. 97). (Step one.)

R moves forward into right *zenkutsu dachi* and attacks with *chudan tsuki*, while simultaneously **L** moves back into left *zenkutsu dachi* and blocks left *chudan soto uke* (Fig. 98). (Step two.)

R moves forward into left *zenkutsu dachi* and attacks with left *gedan tsuki*, while simultaneously **L** moves back into right *zenkutsu dachi* and blocks right *gedan barai* (Fig. 99). (Step three.)

In the same position and stance, **L** immediately counter-attacks with a left *chudan gyaku tsuki* (Fig. 100) and covers in preparation for a block (Fig. 101) and executes a right *mae gedan barai* (Fig. 102) which completes the sequence.

Again, this sequence can be repeated with **R** taking the attacking role and **L** the defensive role.

Once competent in these forms, the student can quite easily develop various other combinations.

It is worth noting that constant practice of this method of practice fighting will assist in developing the *Karateka's* timing, focus and technique. Once three step practice fighting has been successfully mastered, the student may wish to try one step practice fighting, in which both your techniques and your partner's are much faster.

Fig.95

Fig.96

Fig.97

Fig.98

Fig.99

Fig.100

Fig.101

Fig.102

Free-style fighting

Ultimately, once all the basic forms of practice fighting have been completed, the student can then move onto **free-style fighting**. It is now that the theory learnt so far can be put into practice. It must be stressed that under no circumstances should free fighting be performed without both the guidance and observation of your instructor.

There are various types of equipment which the student may choose to use during practice fighting. The choice will depend on what is available and what is affordable. Handmits, shin and instep protectors, groin guards, body guards and head guards are generally available but are not always necessary, if practice fighting is of the non-contact type. Much experience and training is necessary within a *dojo* before anyone should consider contact or semi-contact practice fighting, and even when ready, they should only be attempted under the guidance of a qualified instructor. It cannot be emphasised enough that care must be taken at all times to avoid serious injury – you only have one body, so take care of it.

8

Combination Techniques

The Karate student must, of course, recognise the importance of having a sense of physical awareness before attempting to mould into one the many concepts learnt so far. The ability to defend oneself and, indeed, the ability to fight are also vital, for obvious reasons.

By now you will appreciate that, in order to fight effectively, you must be able to rely on many physical and psychological aspects.

Practising combinations

Nearly all forms of fighting arts have methods of practice fighting and in chapter 7 we described the one step and three step versions. This chapter will explain the method of practising combination techniques. It should be appreciated that in practice fighting within the *dojo* or indeed in a real life situation, you would, by sheer necessity, use more than one technique to defend yourself against an opponent. It is generally accepted and indeed realistic that you will be unable to stop an opponent by using just a single punch or strike. You would probably require a series of techniques to enable you to overcome your opponent or attacker.

To this end it is advisable to practise a set series of blocks and counter-attacks of varying degrees of complexity, depending on your level of ability. In order to assist the development of position, balance, co-ordination, form, speed, power and reflex in a defensive and counter-attacking situation, the practice of combinations is extremely useful.

It is worth remembering that it is generally neither possible nor realistic to plan a strategy for every situation. Practising combination techniques will give you the confidence and ability to defend and counter-attack in an effective and efficient manner rather than relying on a 'stop, start' process which would not be effective.

Ultimately, the combination sequences which you have learnt will prove to be practical and worthwhile, especially as your experience and knowledge of different techniques grow.

This chapter explains a few combinations which can be practised either on your own or with a partner if you need to practise focus; you will realise that gradually they become more complicated. Do not be afraid to add to these general examples or to insert different techniques. Indeed, use these examples as a starting point from which to build and try to develop your own ideas and more importantly practise what you feel works for you given your physical situation and ability.

Combination no. 1

From a right fighting position (Fig. 103), cover with your right hand and kick *chudan mae geri* (Fig. 104). Land with your right leg in front (Fig. 105) and immediately strike with a *chudan gyaku tsuki* (Fig. 106) and finally return to the fighting position (Fig. 107).

Fig.103

Fig.104

Fig.105

Fig.106

Fig.107

Combination no. 2

From a left fighting position (Fig. 108), slide forward and block an imaginary punch with *chudan soto uke* (Fig. 109). With the same arm, block either an imaginary punch or kick to the groin with *mae gedan barai* (Fig. 110), immediately counter-attack with a right *chudan gyaku tsuki* (Fig. 111) and return to your fighting position (Fig. 112).

Fig.108

Fig.109

Fig.110

Fig.111

Fig.112

Combination no. 3

From a left fighting position (Fig. 113), cover with your right hand and kick *chudan mae geri* (Fig. 114). Land forward with your right foot and immediately kick with your left leg a *chudan yoko geri* (Fig. 115). Land with your left leg forward and then turn your body and *kick ushiro geri* (Fig. 116). Land forward with your right leg into a fighting position and strike *chudan gyaku tsuki* (Fig. 117). Immediately return to a fighting position (Fig. 118).

Fig.113

Fig.115

Fig.114

Fig.116

Fig.117

Fig.118

Combination no. 4

From a left fighting position (Fig. 119), slide back and block an imaginary kick to the groin with a *mae gedan barai* (Fig. 120). Immediately strike with a left *ago uchi* (Fig. 121) and a *chudan gyaku tsuki* (Fig. 122). Move your right leg through (Fig. 123) and position yourself to kick left *chudan mae geri* (Fig. 124). Land forward with your left foot and with your right leg kick *jodan mawashi geri* (Fig. 125). Land forward with your right foot and position yourself for, and execute, a left *ushiro geri* (Fig. 126). Land in a left fighting position (Fig. 127) and block an imaginary attack to the groin (Fig. 128). Immediately counter-attack with a right *chudan gyaku tsuki* (Fig. 129) and return to a fighting position (Fig. 130).

Fig.119

Fig.120

Fig.121

Fig.122

Fig.123

Fig.124

Fig.125

Fig.126

Fig.127

Fig.128

Fig.129

Fig.130

9

Kata

What is *kata*?

The performance of *kata* enables the student to practise the basic fundamental aspects of Karate, either with fellow members of a club or individually. The practice obviously involves many techniques and methods of movement, and the constant diligent performance of *kata* will eventually give the student a good all round means of exercise and muscle development.

It may be helpful to think of the individual techniques explained in earlier chapters (i.e. strikes, kicks and blocks) as essentially the 'alphabet of Karate', or the individual elements which when combined make up Karate.

Kata is an extension of this and can be seen as a means of combining many of these techniques and thus of giving them a form – *kata* could be described as 'the spelling that forms the words and sentences from the Karate alphabet'.

Kata is primarily a form of exercise using various Karate techniques. In its basic form, *kata* consists of a predetermined series of techniques performed in a set sequence.

There are many aspects to *kata*, and unfortunately space permits only an introduction to the basics of the exercise. Since *kata* is composed of so many different elements, it is advisable to train with and seek the guidance of an instructor if you want to perfect the technique.

If you examine closely the various techniques practised in *kata*, you will discover an adaptability of these techniques within which a system of self-defence can develop. In addition you may also want to develop and adapt certain techniques and apply them to a fighting situation. Remember that *kata* is fundamentally a means of both practising and remembering techniques and, in addition, a means of developing a disciplined mind and body. It is not, as is sometimes remarked, a method of fighting many opponents. In order to advance in both the learning and basic understanding of *kata*, the student will need to take a number of progressive steps and will have to possess a general understanding of the basic exercises involved in each *kata*.

The ingredients of *kata*

The progressive steps of development and learning are the same as those for Karate as a whole – for easy reference, they are summarised again below:

(a) **Position**
The student should have a good theoretical and practical knowledge of all Karate stances and techniques.
(b) **Balance**
This is the means by which the student controls the actual body position both stationary and in movement.
(c) **Co-ordination**
This enables the student to execute various techniques with controlled balance in a given position.
(d) **Form**
The student can develop form by executing all techniques with good position, balance and co-ordination.
(e) **Speed**
This is where the student increases the rhythm of performance without any loss of form.
(f) **Power**
The strengthening of the techniques of the *kata*.

(g) **Reflex**

Having successfully understood and developed all the above steps, the student will reach a stage, through constant repetition, whereby the techniques become a natural movement.

In Karate, it is important to shift your weight from one foot to another whilst performing an attack or defence, and at the same time maintain your balance. In addition, you must be able to inject maximum power into a leg or foot whilst kicking or striking, so it is essential to master split second timing.

Ultimately, you will be able to amalgamate the seven elements described above.

The first *kata* generally learnt at a *dojo* follows the pattern as set out below. The name of this *kata* varies, and there are a few differences from karate style to karate style, but the basic *kata* is called *Taikyoku Sono Ichi*. *Taikyoku kata* was brought together by the late Karate master, Gichin Funakoshi, and it combines basic lower parries or blocks with middle level punches. It was originally intended for beginners, but its excellence as an exercise has led to popularity among advanced students as well.

How to approach the *kata*

Firstly, attempt to memorise the techniques and stances in easily manageable sections – do not attempt to learn the whole sequence in one go because you will only succeed in confusing yourself. While you are learning the *kata* do not lose heart – try not to give in to its apparent complexity. After a few hours you will be surprised how easy it becomes.

Start by learning the sequence from Figure 131 to Figure 136. Once you have succeeded in doing that, move on to the sequence shown in Figure 137 to Figure 139, but return to Figure 131 each time, so that you repeat the whole sequence gradually.

Once you have become proficient at this *kata*, you should aim to complete the whole sequence in between 20 and 30 seconds.

The student should not rush the learning process and, as far as possible, should establish and understand each individual movement within a *kata*. In addition he or she should take care to understand the actual meaning of the technique being performed and not perform the *kata* in appearance form only.

In your constant practice of *kata* you must attempt to achieve the **impossible, which is perfection. You should not be deterred from** striving for this seemingly unobtainable goal and, in doing so, you should put your whole body and mind into the performance of *kata*, as you would in the other aspects of your Karate training.

Taikyoku Sono Ichi

Start the *kata* in *fudo dachi* (Fig. 131).

Bring both hands open to ear height, palms facing inwards, simultaneously position both heels in an outward direction into *uchi-hachi-ji-dachi* (Fig. 132) (NB, these movements are executed quickly). Slowly and with power, bring both hands down clenching them into a fist and at the same time pull both feet in parallel to each other into *yoi dachi* (Fig. 133).

Move your left foot at 90° to the left (Fig. 134) into *zenkutsu dachi* and block *mae gedan barai* (Fig. 135) (NB, ensure that your left fist is approximately 'one fist' space above your left knee).

Move forward into right *zenkutsu dachi* and punch right *chudan oi tsuki* (Fig. 136).

With your right foot, slide diagonally backwards placing your right foot in the correct position and at the same time positioning your arms ready for the block (Fig. 137). Turn your body at the completion of the movement 180° into right *zenkutsu dachi* and block *mae gedan barai* (Fig. 138).

Move forward into left *zenkutsu dachi* and punch left *chudan oi tsuki* (Fig. 139).

Move your left foot at 90° (Fig. 140) into left *zenkutsu dachi* and block *mae gedan barai* (Fig. 141).

Move forward into right *zenkutsu dachi* and punch right *chudan oi tsuki* (Fig. 142).

Move forward into left *zenkutsu dachi* and punch left *chudan oi tsuki* (Fig. 143).

Move forward into right *zenkutsu dachi*, punch right *chudan oi tsuki* and *kiai* (Fig. 144).

Move the left foot at 90° and pivot on the right foot (Fig. 145) into left *zenkutsu dachi* and block *mae gedan barai* (Fig. 146).

Move forward into right *zenkutsu dachi* and punch right *chudan oi tsuki* (Fig. 147).

Move the right foot back turning the body 180° (Fig. 148) into right *zenkutsu dachi* and block *mae gedan barai* (Fig. 149).

Move forward into left *zenkutsu dachi* and punch left *chudan oi tsuki* (Fig. 150).

Move the left foot at 90° (Fig. 151) into left *zenkutsu dachi* and block *mae gedan barai* (Fig. 152).

Move forward into right *zenkutsu dachi* and punch right *chudan oi tsuki* (Fig. 153).

Move forward into left *zenkutsu dachi* and punch left *chudan oi tsuki* (Fig. 154).

Move forward into right *zenkutsu dachi*, punch left *chudan oi tsuki* and *kiai* (Fig. 155).

Move the left foot at 90° (Fig. 156) into left *zenkutsu dachi* and block *mae gedan barai* (Fig. 157).

Move forward into right *zenkutsu dachi* and punch right *chudan oi tsuki* (Fig. 158).

Move the right foot back turning the body 180° (Fig. 159) into right *zenkutsu dachi* and block *mae gedan barai* (Fig. 160).

Move forward into left *zenkutsu dachi* and punch left *chudan oi tsuki* (Fig. 161).

To complete the *kata* move the left foot into *fudo dachi* (Figs 162 to 163).

A translation of terminology in order of occurrence:

1	*Fudo Dachi*	Formal stance
2	*Uchi Hachi Ji Dachi*	Figure of eight stance
3	*Yoi Dachi*	Ready stance
4	*Zenkutsu Dachi*	Forward leaning stance
5	*Mae Gedan Barai*	Lower parry or block
6	*Chudan Oi Tsuki*	Middle level thrust punch
7	*Kiai*	Shout

Fig.131 Fudo Dachi

Fig.132

Fig.133

Fig.134

Fig.135 Mae Gedan Barai

Fig.136 Chudan Oi Tsuki

Fig.137

Fig.138 Mae Gedan Barai

Fig.139 Chudan Oi Tsuki

Fig.140

Fig.141 Mae Gedan Barai

Fig.142 Chudan Oi Tsuki

Fig.143 Chudan Oi Tsuki

Fig.144 Chudan Oi Tsuki

Fig.145

Fig.146 Mae Gedan Barai

Fig.147 Chudan Oi Tsuki

Fig.148

Fig.149 Mae Gedan Barai

Fig.150 Chudan Oi Tsuki

Fig.151

Fig.152 Mae Gedan Barai

Fig.153 Chudan Oi Tsuki

Fig.154 Chudan Oi Tsuki

Fig.155 Chudan Oi Tsuki

Fig.156

Fig.157 Mae Gedan Barai

Fig.158 Chudan Oi Tsuki

Fig.159

Fig.160 Mae Gedan Barai

Fig.161 Chudan Oi Tsuki

Fig.162

Fig.163 Fudo Dachi

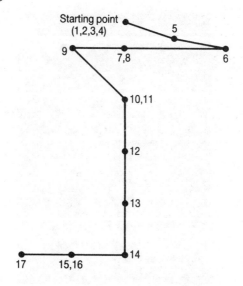

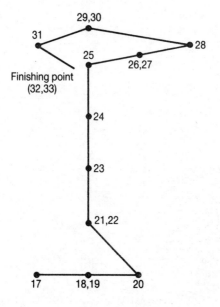

Fig.164

10

Karate Tournaments

- Karate as a martial art
- Competitive Karate
- Contact tournaments
- Non-contact tournaments

Karate as a martial art

Martial arts have developed throughout the centuries and it is worth remembering that, in its final analysis, Karate is an 'art of fighting', as it was in samurai times. Should we ever lose sight of this fact, there is the danger that Karate as a martial art will cease to exist. We must not forget that Karate has developed as a means of defeating an opponent in a real and practical situation.

There are certain Karate organisations today which specialise in teaching 'sport Karate' and in doing so cater for a specific need. Sport Karate is geared towards not only training the body, developing stamina and physical endurance, but also towards participation in tournaments.

'Sport Karate' organisations in general place no emphasis on the spiritual and deeper teachings of Karate masters, since they choose to concentrate on the sporting aspects.

There *are* Karate organisations which do involve themselves to a greater extent in the *budo* aspect of Karate, that is in the teachings fundamental to the martial art.

A literal translation of *budo* is *bu*, meaning 'war', and *do* meaning 'way', so *budo* can be translated as 'the way of war'. But conversely it is possible to translate the Japanese character *bu* as 'cease the struggle'.

Budo Karate teaches you to become strong and can give enlightenment and wisdom with the help of a good instructor.

It is also important that Karate should be seen as a lifelong challenge. Within this period of time you will pursue not only physical perfection and excellence as far as possible, but also strive for spiritual perfection. Masutatsu Oyama (10th Dan), one of the world's greatest living Karate masters, has said that in his or her youth the *karateka* should place emphasis more on strength and power and that, as the years progress and his or her strength fades, the *karateka* will concentrate more on technique and spiritual teachings. In light of this the discovery of Karate is open to people of all ages and generations from six to sixty and far beyond.

Competitive Karate

Yet Karate today has, in general, geared itself towards the competitive arena. On one hand it is possible to argue that Karate has only one purpose, in that your goal should be to pursue as far as possible the development of spirit and body. If this is the case, it should only be studied as a martial art.

On the other hand it can be argued that, although Karate is primarily a martial art, it can be regarded as a sport, in terms of competitions and tournaments. Before the advent of the martial art movies, it was no doubt tournaments and demonstrations which brought Karate to the public eye, and encouraged many people to follow it.

There are many people who believe that there is no room for tournaments within martial arts, and conversely there are those who say that tournaments are an essential part of the progression of Karate.

Whatever your own viewpoint, it is a fact that many tournaments are held throughout the world at club, regional, national and international level and that they have helped, and will continue to help, the spread of popularity of Karate throughout the world.

It is debatable whether a student's performance in a competition is a fair reflection of his or her ability because each tournament has its own rules and regulations, and the fighters will be wearing some form of protective equipment.

There are two main types of tournaments: contact and non-contact. In the various non-contact type of tournaments there are different forms of match.

Contact tournaments
On one hand there are contact tournaments, whereby contestants score points, as in boxing, to win the match or else win by knocking out their opponent. Examples of these are full contact, kick boxing and knockdown tournaments. The rules for each tournament differ slightly, as do the rules about what sort of protective equipment can be worn – but in all systems the attacks are full contact.

Non-contact tournaments
On the other hand we have the *WUKO* system, where fighters score points or half points for single techniques, and win by accumulating three full points. Alternatively, there is a multiple scoring competition, where the fighters compete for two minutes and the judges give points for scoring techniques; at the end of the match the points are totalled to decide the winner. There are also various forms of semi-contact systems following similar rules.

Fig.165

11

Fitness and Stamina Training

A person's fitness and stamina are determined by his or her age and physical ability. In all martial arts you must develop a level of fitness which will enable you to perform what you have learnt without a drastic loss of skill due to tiredness or exhaustion. During practice fighting, and indeed during basic training, the student must be able to maintain a high work rate and also must have a quick recovery rate. In order to be able to achieve these two requirements the student should work at becoming fit. Care must be taken here, as you should remember that fitness must never be seen as a substitute for Karate ability or skill – the two things are complementary.

Through the many years of martial arts training, there are traditional ways of becoming fitter. Each year there is an advance in fitness theory and methods which is due in part to a questioning and improvement of traditional methods.

There are many different areas of fitness which the *karateka* should attempt to improve and the following is a list of the main ones:

(a) Cardiovascular efficiency
(b) Respiratory efficiency
(c) Muscle endurance
(d) Power
(e) Speed
(f) Flexibility

Your understanding and knowledge of these areas of fitness will develop as you progress through your martial arts career.

As mentioned earlier, the aim is for a level of fitness which will enable the satisfactory performance of various tasks without a loss of skill, due to, for example, tiredness, breathlessness, an aching body, weakness, slowness and perhaps stiffness.

It is strongly advised that anyone embarking on Karate training for the first time should seek medical advice before beginning to test his or her body. This will clearly depend on the individual's age and general health, but it is always an idea to have a check-up anyway. In the early stages of your Karate career it would be sensible not to concentrate too heavily on the fitness aspect of your training but use it to supplement your karate training.

Obviously one method of improving your general level of fitness is by running or skipping. Again there are many types of running training, depending on the distance, speed and frequency of the run. You will benefit from running in many ways, most noticeably in terms of endurance and speed of recovery.

It would be advisable to begin on a short run, say half a mile, at a moderate pace, in order to establish your level of fitness. In the following weeks or months, progress slowly and carefully to longer runs at a greater speed, varying your tempo with intermittent sprint runs.

Fitness can also be improved by a sensible programme of weight training which again will supplement your Karate training.

In an earlier chapter we mentioned some conditioning exercises such as push ups, sit ups and squats. These exercises can be used on their own, but can also be incorporated into a circuit, whereby you repeat the task in a given number of sets or over a given period of time.

It is possible to do circuits individually or in groups and they are ideal in the sense that you can fit the exercises to your individual needs. You can, for example, do 10 of each exercise for three sets (i.e. do 10 push ups, three times, with a rest between each set of ten). Alternatively, you can perform each exercise for a given period of time (e.g. 30 seconds) for three sets, attempting to improve your performance as the weeks pass.

Below is a guide to a possible circuit which you may wish to follow and even improve on:

(i)   Push ups (Fig. 7, pages 28–29)
(ii) Standing jumps (Fig. 166, page 166)
(iii) Sit ups (Fig. 8, pages 30–31)
(iv) Burpees (Fig. 167, pages 166–167)
(v)   Leg raises (Fig. 168, page 168)

Remember to warm up and stretch your muscles thoroughly before starting your training in order to avoid injuring yourself.

Finally, once you have joined a club your instructor will be able to assist and advise you on a more comprehensive programme to improve your fitness relative to your own ability.

Fig.166

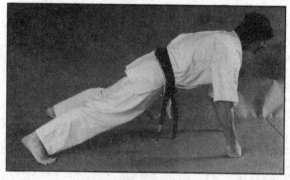

Fig.167a

Fig.167b

Fig.167c

12

Self-Defence

The concept of self-defence

One of the most important concepts of Karate training is avoiding conflict and daily training will assist you in this. In order to avoid being caught up in conflict, the *karateka*'s spiritual attitude is of utmost importance.

The fact remains however, that in present day society, violence and unrest are all about us. We have no idea when we may confront a situation which will put us in danger, so we must be constantly aware and should not be negligent in our training. A person who is capable of protecting him- or herself can maintain a natural spiritual attitude. In light of this fact it is necessary to study and learn self-defence techniques, because they are a vital element of your overall martial arts training. These techniques are additional to your basic Karate training. If an opponent attacks you, you must be confident and efficient in your use of the Karate techniques which you practise. Should the situation arise where your Karate techniques are not practical, the self-defence techniques will in many situations be more effective.

Daily practice of techniques is essential, even if you only know one or two techniques. It should be your ultimate aim to be able to apply the technique speedily and accurately, whilst at the same time remaining calm. For any of the following techniques to be effective, they must be practised over a long period of time under the guidance of your instructor. In actually using these techniques, the element of surprise will contribute to the overall success of the manoeuvre.

The self-defence techniques illustrated below are very basic and easy to use and learn, but they can also be extremely effective.

Self-defence application no. 1

Your opponent grabs your wrist as in Figure 169 (right hand to left wrist). This hold can be broken by pulling and twisting your left arm towards your right ear, working on your opponent's weakness, i.e. the thumb and finger (as in Fig. 170). NB This is the same as the initial hand position when bringing the arm up in preparation for a *gedan barai* block.

As the grip is broken, you can follow with a strike (*uraken*) to your opponent's face (Fig. 171), and immediately follow with a punch (*gyaku tsuki*) (Fig. 172).

Fig. 169

Fig.170

Fig.171

Fig.172

Self-defence application no. 2

Your opponent grabs your wrist as in Figure 173 (right hand to left wrist). Turn anti-clockwise to your opponent (i.e. with your back towards him or her), grabbing your opponent's right arm and twisting your own left arm at the same time (Fig. 174). Then pull your opponent's arm tight into your back and, gripping it firmly, strike with your right fist (*tettsui*) or any other suitable striking technique (Fig. 175). The initial leg movement is similar to the unorthodox turn in *Taikyoku Sono Ichi*, after the third step and *kiai* – see chapter 9 for this).

Fig.173

Fig.174

Fig.175

Self-defence application no. 3

Your opponent grabs your lapel as in Figure 176 (right hand to
left side). Bring your left arm over your opponent's holding arm and
position your right hand ready for a strike (Fig. 177). While pushing
your left arm down on your opponent's arm, thus breaking his or her
balance, complete the technique by striking right *tettsui komekami*
(Fig. 178).

Fig.176

Fig.177

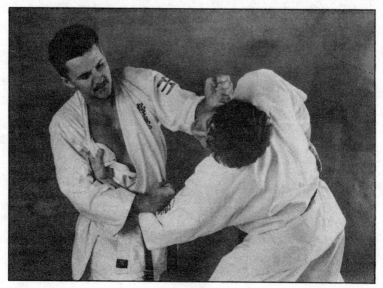

Fig.178

Self-defence application no. 4

Your opponent grabs your left lapel as shown in Figure 179, immediately seize from underneath his or her wrist with your left hand (Fig. 180), then step through with your left leg at the same time turning away from your opponent and reinforce your hold with your right hand bringing your attacker's arm onto your shoulder (Fig. 181). To complete the combination, bend your knees and at the same time pull the arm down, thus exerting leverage (Fig. 182).

Fig.179

Fig.180

Fig.181

Fig.182

Self-defence application no. 5

Your opponent has grabbed hold of your right shoulder or lapel with his or her left hand (Fig. 183).

Bring your left hand to his or her hand and grip it from above (Fig. 184).

Simultaneously, swing your right arm around on top of your opponent's elbow from the outside. Down your opponent by adding a spring movement with your hips at the same time as you put downward pressure on his or her elbow diagonally to the left (Fig. 185).

Fig.184

Fig.185

Glossary of Terms

Japanese commands used in the *dojo*

Naore	Return to original position
Yame	Stop
Yoi	Get ready
Mogare	No counting
Hajime	Begin
Mawatte	Turn
Kamaete	Perform the technique
Hidari	Left
Migi	Right
Ushiro	Rear
Ippon Kumite	One step fighting
Sanbon Kumite	Three step fighting

Counting in Japanese

Ichi	1
Ni	2
San	3
Shi	4
Go	5
Roku	6
Shichi	7
Hachi	8
Ku	9
Ju	10

Some terms used in Karate

Age Hiji Ate	Rising elbow strike
Ago Uchi	Jaw strike
Ashi Barai	Foot sweep
Barai	Sweep
Budo	Martial way
Chudan Tsuki	Middle thrust
Chudan Uke	Middle block
Chusoku	Ball of the foot
Dachi	Stance
Dan	Black belt grade
Fudo Dachi	Formal stance
Ganmen Uchi	Strike to the face
Gedan	Lower
Gedan Barai	Lower block
Gedan Tsuki	Lower thrust
Geri (Mae Geri)	Kick
Gyaku	Opposite
Haisoku	Instep
Haito	Inner knife hand
Heiko Dachi	Parallel stance
Heisoku Dachi	Parallel closed stance
Hiji	Elbow
Hiraken	Flat fist
Hirate	Flat hand
Hiza Geri	Knee kick
Hizo Uchi	Spleen strike
Ibuki	Method of breathing
Ippon	One
Jodan Tsuki	Upper thrust
Jodan Uke	Upper block
Juji	Cross
Kakato	Heel
Kake	Hook
Kake Dachi	Hook stance
Kansetsu Geri	Joint kick
Kara	Empty
Kata	Formal exercise
Keiko	Chicken beak hand
Kiai	Shout
Kiba Dachi	Straddle stance

Kihon	Basic
Kin Geri	Groin kick
Koken	Bent wrist
Kokutsu Dachi	Back leaning stance
Komekami	Temple
Kote	Forearm
Kumite	Fighting
Mae Geri	Forward kick
Mawashi Geri	Roundhouse kick
Mawashi Uchi	Roundhouse strike
Mawashi Uke	Roundhouse block
Mokuso	Meditation
Moroashi Dachi	One foot forward stance
Morote	Both hands
Musubi Dachi	Open toes stance
Nekoashi Dachi	Cat stance
Nihon Nukite	Two finger spear
Nogare	Method of breathing
Nukite	Spear hand
Oroshi	Descending strike
Oyayubi	Thumb
Ryutoken	Dragon's head fist
Sakotsu Uchi	Strike to the collarbone
Sayu	Left and right
Seiken	Forefist
Shita	Lower
Shotei	Palm heel
Shuto	Knife hand
Sokuto	Knife foot
Soto	Outside
Te	Hand
Teisoku	Arch
Tettsui	Fist-edge
Tobi	Jump
Toho	Sword-peak hand
Tsuki	Punch
Tsuruashi Dachi	Crane stance
Uchi	Strike or inside
Uchi Komi	Strike forward
Uchi Hachi Ji Dachi	Figure of eight stance
Uke	Block
Ura	Reverse

Uraken	Inverted fist strike
Ushiro	Back or behind
Yoko	Side
Zenkutsu Dachi	Forward leaning stance

TEACH YOURSELF BOOKS

SQUASH

Revised by Ian McKenzie
including the complete Rules of Squash

This extremely lucid guide to one of today's most popular sports takes the budding squash player from the game's origins through the basic techniques and shots to the more advanced areas of match play. The authors discuss each stroke in detail with the help of clear illustrations and photographs, and move on to discuss the psychology of the match.

The official Rules of Squash and advice on court etiquette and fitness are also included in this invaluable guide to improving and enjoying your squash.

TEACH YOURSELF BOOKS

GOLF

Current Ryder Cup Captain, Bernard Gallacher and Mark Wilson

includes the complete, revised Rules of Golf

Are you a complete beginner, a leisurely weekend golfer or do you participate in competition matches? Whatever your skills, handicap or experience, this book will help you to improve and enjoy your game. The golfer is taken step by step from choosing a set of clubs to playing the more complex bunker shots and awkward lies. A particularly helpful section discusses the identification and eradication of common faults. The book is illustrated throughout and includes the complete, revised Rules of Golf, as approved by the Royal and Ancient Golf Club of St. Andrews and the United States Golf Association.

An invaluable guide for those who wish to get the most out of this ever-popular sport.

TEACH YOURSELF BOOKS

JUDO

Syd Hoare

This is a comprehensive guide to judo which will interest and benefit the beginner and Black belt alike. There is a wealth of information on how traditional and modern judo techniques are performed and on how they provide training in both mental and physical development.

The book also contains advice on self-defence, the sources and philosophy of judo and hints on how to prepare for competitions.

The author, Syd Hoare, is one of the most experienced judomen in the UK, and holds the rank of Black belt, 7th Dan. He has trained many young people for the Olympics.